I0140996

To

_____

From

_____

Affirmations
for
Wellness

A Way to Write Affirmations to Heal Body, Mind, and Soul

Affirmations help adjust attitudes toward life: sickness, disease, death, mental health, injury, self-esteem, relationships, and your ever-changing role in life.

To celebrate the joys in life, one at a time, one day at a time:

PRICELESS

Affirmations for Wellness: A Way to Write Affirmations to Heal Body, Mind, and Soul
By Sharon Slemons © 2018

All rights reserved. Use of any part of this publication, whether reproduced, transmitted in any form or by any means, electronic, mechanical, photocopying, recording, or otherwise, or stored in a retrieval system, without the prior consent of the publisher, is an infringement of copyright law and is forbidden.

While the publisher and author have used their best efforts in preparing this book, they make no representations or warranties with respect to the accuracy or completeness of this book and specifically disclaim any implied warranties of merchantability or fitness for a particular purpose.

No warranty may be created or extended by sales representatives or written sales materials. The advice and strategies contained herein may not be suitable for your situation. You should consult with a professional where appropriate. Neither the publisher nor the author shall be liable for any loss of profit or any other commercial damages, including but not limited to special, incidental, consequential, or other damages. The stories and interviews in this book are true although the names and identifiable information may have been changed to maintain confidentiality.

The publisher and author shall have neither liability nor responsibility to any person or entity with respect to loss, damage, or injury caused or alleged to be caused directly or indirectly by the information contained in this book. The information presented herein is in no way intended as a substitute for counseling or other professional guidance.

Print ISBN: 978-1-7325464-0-0
eBook ISBN: 978-1-7325464-1-7

Cover Design: Marina Alcoser
Interior Design: Adriel Wiggins

To order more copies, email sslemons07@gmail.com or order from Amazon.com

Published by Boise Affirmations LLC
Printed in the United States of America

To my younger sister Kathleen
(Slemons) Lee whose "heavenly" guidance is deeply appreciated

(Okay, 93 percent of the time)

Kathy Lee School of Dance

Boise, Idaho, 1973-1997

Introduction

This book is about writing simple yet sometimes powerful statements to and for yourself. During times of fear, anxiety, and stress, we all need to remind ourselves to guide our attitudes in a positive, heartwarming way.

When I was diagnosed with breast cancer on November 30, 2017, I began writing positive quotes, sayings, poems, and jokes to redirect my attitude toward healing. I didn't know what else to do.

I didn't want to make this diagnosis worse by allowing fear, self-pity, or terror to overwhelm me, so when fears slugged into my mind, I was able to identify what I was feeling. I started simple affirmations in my mind like, "May I be healthy, may I be happy, may I be peaceful," repeating it 10-plus times and then starting another affirmation. I just kept going with these running through my mind.

Soon I was writing these in a notebook with felt markers in varying bright colors throughout the pages. The colors alone were inspiring and uplifting.

My only objective was to keep my thinking in a positive, affirming space. The last thing I needed was negativity.

I found that first making a list of the things I was grateful for gave me a starting point for my affirmations. I invite you to join me in writing affirmations for yourself for two weeks, with a goal of writing 50-100 daily. Make time to do this for *you.* The CHOICE IS YOURS!

"When every person in the world takes better care of themselves,
Everyone in the world will feel better taken care of
And then we may finally begin to care more about each other."

—Spencer Johnson, One Minute for Myself

Peaceful blessings to each of you.

You matter to me,

Sharon Slemons

List those things that calm you and things you are thankful for. Maybe it's a person, place, thing, and/or emotion. Use these as a starting point to write your own affirmations. Use mine, offered to you for inspiration, if they help you.

Gratitude List

Writing Affirmations

Suggestions for beginning: choose a color and start writing some of these. Try changing a word or two to make them more your own. Soon you will "spin off" to writing just for yourself.

This is a quiet treasure for you—and you deserve it!

1. Pain of every color stretches me to my very core

2. My best self is honored by my quality choices

3. My aching heart is warming in sky-blue pink clouds

4. I am blessed with calmness

5. I honor our victims of violence. I commit to living in action, goodness, and respect in their honor.

6. I accept the sacred privilege of aging gracefully

7. Prayer, the world's greatest wireless connection

8. Dark fluffy clouds rumbled off with my anger

9. May I have the courage to say NO

10. God's light warms my heart

11. I am healing, this is good!

12. "Look to nature for nurturing. It is as reliable as our God who provides it."

(From Keep-Life-Simple Therapy by Linus Mundy (Abbey Press, 1993))

13. With time and patience, my grief is lessening

14. I am grateful for these painful feelings, I'm healing

15. My future is safe and secure with God

16. At this moment everything IS all right

17. I love each of us for our very real humanness

1. Having a positive attitude is a precious jewel indeed

2. My inner child is calm, yet sensitive

3. May I find peace today, in spite of challenges I face

4. Changing my thoughts creates abundance for me

5. God tells me I am welcomed, deserving, adored

6. My soul is enriched in our great outdoors

7. Only kindness makes sense

8. May I connect with goodness and health

9. My body, mind, and spirit are in perfect harmony

10. Don't outrun your guardian angel!

11. Forgiveness fosters humility which invites gratitude

12. It is freeing to let go

13. Bubbly laughter from some of our sickest—what JOY!

14. I treat myself with gentleness, kindness, and compassion

15. I pay attention to this "present" moment

16. Abundance flows freely in all areas of my life!

1. I will step up to help our mentally ill

2. My strength and resiliency grow through my PTSD

3. God's goodness totally surrounds me

4. Thank You, God, for my courage to "let go"

5. I choose to no longer drip in self-pity

6. Our shooting tragedy on February 14, 2018, at Stoneman Douglas H.S., Parkland, Florida, ignited dynamic change in me.

(This was a turning point for me personally.)

7. Collecting smiles is life at its best!

8. I am deeply grateful for a good day!

9. People listen with their eyes—my smile is talking!

10. My aching heart encourages my recovery from tragedy

11. Take care of your heart, it's God's garden

12. God blesses me beautifully, especially when I'm out of my comfort zone—like today—now

13. It's such a JOY to LIVE WELL!

14. My life has changed; I observe with patience

15. I intend to receive universal abundance

16. I am my own personal hero

1. The marchers' convictions thrill me! Change is rolling in on the shoulders of our teenagers. I am humbly proud.

(High school students demanded change in mental health and gun control on March 14, 2018, through a walkout, one month after the Parkland, Florida, shooting.)

2. I refresh my spirit in the fresh spring air

3. I listen to the wisdom of our YOUNG ONES

4. This flickering candle calms and soothes me deeply

5. My soul is enriched with powerful waters saying "go with the flow;" with pure air enticing me to breathe deeply; with a solid earth rooting me in stability.

6. Every day I picture myself content and happy

7. Their loving support kindles fresh enthusiasm!

8. I awake to our uniting spirits

9. My body heals as I engage in right thinking

10. I believe the light of God surrounds me:

I believe I am cancer-FREE
I believe I have purpose
I believe I am loved
I believe I AM WORTHY!

1. I take life more calmly, knowing all is well at this moment

2. Communication = language of the heart

   (From Bill W.'s Grapevine Writings, The Language of the Heart (The AA Grapevine, 1988))

3. With deep love, I let _____ go

4. My life promises goodness, safety, and peace

5. I trust the gift of change that comes with pain

6. I choose to make today a pleasure to experience

7. I think thoughts of attraction for a healthy, comfortable life of quality

8. Giving and receiving attention is my life's blessing

9. Abundance of the universe surrounds and protects me

10. I invite loving behavior by giving it

11. I push the boundaries outside my comfort zone

12. The warm sunshine is just what I needed

13. Praise softens. I smile from within.

14. Love is having/giving the experience that I/you matter!

15. I am dedicated to my recovery—spiritual, physical, and emotional

1. This is the best and most loving thing I do for myself

2. God takes care of me in my unknown

3. Let's live how we dance—HAPPY!

4. I am AWESOMELY WELL!

5. Changing my thoughts makes me feel GOOD

6. I surrender my fears, grief, and anger

7. Negativity melts as I receive universal blessings

8. I am FREE of all negative emotions

9. I anticipate goodness

10. I am cancer-FREE!

11. I bring God's goodness wherever I am

12. It's comforting to know we don't need to take any step alone

13. Thank you for my anger showing me that I'm hurting

14. I have everything I need to take care of myself

15. Today is a gift we call "the present"

16. Perfect health never came from comfort zones!

17. Giving grows the heart

1. I know the Spirit is as close as my thoughts, my breath

2. Today will be joyful with lots of sweet laughter

3. I am privileged to live in this wonderous body

4. LIVE INTENTIONALLY

5. Thank You, God, for each person in my life

6. As I honor my spirit, I am safe—secure

7. To live boldly, I say, I'm not done yet!

8. I choose to be healthy and FREE

9. I willingly receive goodness

10. I believe my life is abundant in all ways!

11. Dear God, please take each person who helps avert violent tragedy into Your arms and love them dearly

12. I intentionally declare a happy, peaceful day!

13. My inner self appreciates pampering and praise

14. Thank You, God, for a preciously good day!

15. Dear God, thank You for my ability to be grateful for goodness in the midst of cancer treatment—I am truly blessed!

1. Dear God, please bless my fears and anxieties that I may appreciate today more fully

2. God's loving white light purifies my every thought

3. May I appreciate the grieving involved in letting go

4. I am grateful for my friend _____

5. I deeply appreciate my healthy, safe, cancer recovery

6. I release the past; I am FREE to move forward with LOVE in my heart

7. My mind is clear; full of loving white light of LOVE

8. I AM disease-FREE

9. God grant me the strength to love my best and never fear my worst

10. I think perfect thoughts

11. I gratefully accept offers of help as needed

12. Laugh, laugh, laugh! Thank You for my healing

13. I concentrate on my gifts of love, given and received

14. It's a blissful peace given freely by the universe

1. Love soothes, inspires, and enhances my wholeness

2. I am Divinely guided and protected

3. God directs my beliefs, thoughts, and actions when I let Him

4. I ask God's blessing as I step away from being a caregiver

5. God please bless the "not nice" people in my life

6. I believe in respect. I believe in letting go. I believe in goodness. I believe in listening. I believe in compassion.

7. I celebrate WELLNESS!

8. I am relaxed, centered and peaceful; I am strong and secure

9. I am doing what I couldn't do—let go of _____

10. I think caring thoughts about special people, sending an angel to watch over them

11. May I be gracious and kind today

12. I value the person I am becoming

13. Letting go—focus my attention on NOW. I trust that goodness eases this process.

14. "Piglet sidled up to Pooh from behind. 'Pooh!' He whispered. 'Yes Piglet?' 'Nothing,' said Piglet, taking Pooh's paw. 'I just wanted to be sure of you.'"

(From The House at Pooh Corner by A.A. Milne (Dutton's Books for Young Readers, 1988))

1. Today I trust the goodness in each of us

2. Acceptance nurtures wisdom-attracting love and joy

3. May I live in a way that allows me to think WELL of myself

4. My forgiving state of mind is a magnetic power for attracting good

5. The universe guides me in all matters of importance today

6. I am totally willing to love myself

7. Happiness is contagious!

8. Live intentionally; have a childlike wonder; and focus on serenity

9. I think about the goodness in my life—I thank the universe for these precious gifts

10. The richness of my life depends on my wholehearted efforts to nurture meaningful relationships

11. I am a happy, joyful being

12. Watch! Someone's eyes are smiling

13. With wisdom comes glimpses of pure wonder

14. Today's blessings bring clarity

A Final Note

I am using my affirmations for all kinds of life's adventures; from family interactions, to maintaining a healthy lifestyle, to making safe and reasonable choices for my future.

Resources

Bill W.'s Grapevine Writings: *The Language of the Heart*. The AA Grapevine, 1988.

Byrne, Rhonda. *The Secret.* Beyond Words Publishing, 2006.

Casey, Karen. *Each Day a New Beginning: Daily Meditations for Women (Hazelden Meditations).* Hazelden Publishing, 1982.

Hay, Louise L. *You Can Heal Your Life.* Hay House, 1987.

Johnson, Spencer. *One Minute for Myself: How to Manage Your Most Valuable Asset.* Avon Books, 1987.

Milne, A. A. *The House at Pooh Corner.* Dutton Books for Young Readers, 1988.

Mundy, Linus. *Keep-Life-Simple Therapy.* One Caring Place Abbey Press, 1993.

Williamson, Marianne. *Illuminata.* Random House, 1994.

Index

Acknowledgments

Marlene and Barb and all the others in their hospital

gowns in the waiting rooms in hospitals everywhere.

*

My niece, Mandy, who checks on me daily.

*

To friends from first grade Linda Davis

and Susan Choate for their quality listening skills

and their enthusiastic feedback.

*

Silver Sneakers classes at Boise Downtown YMCA

with our dynamic instructors

Deanna Graves and Nancy Davis.

*

Maryanna Young and Jennifer Regner

of Aloha Publishing, thank you

for your patience with me

and commitment

to this book.

*

Peaceful Blessings to you all!

About the Author

Sharon is a retired teacher who has worked with elementary and special education students for 34 years. She was raised in Jerome, Idaho, and graduated from Idaho State University with a B.A. in Education. She lives in Boise, Idaho, where she loves walking the greenbelt along the Boise River. She watches for bald eagles, hawks, herons, and deer while listening to the gurgling waters. These walks in the fresh air are an affirmation of her total well-being. It is a quiet and refreshing time.

Her long-time friends and family nurture and inspire her. Sharon writes affirmations to enhance her everyday life. Not only does she compose, write, and reiterate affirmations, she is dedicated to smiling, speaking, and waving to at least 10 people daily.

www.ingramcontent.com/pod-product-compliance
Lightning Source LLC
LaVergne TN
LVHW072112070426
835509LV00003B/124